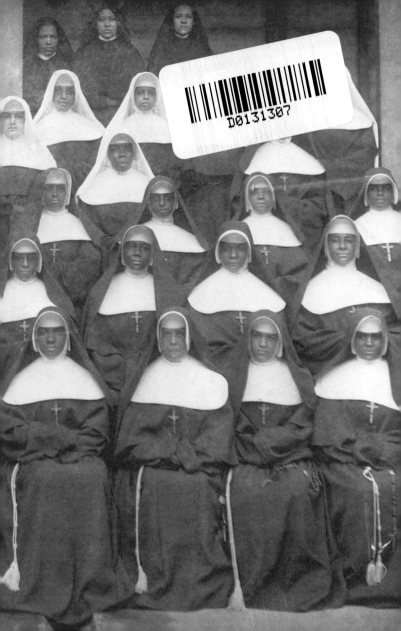

D0131307

Scary Nuns

HarperCollins books may be purchased for educational, business, or sales
promotional use. For information please write: Special Markets Department,
HarperCollins Publishers, 10 East 53rd Street, New York, NY 10022.

FIRST EDITION

Produced by Essential Works
Designer for Essential Works: Barbara Doherty
168a Camden Street, London NW1 9PT, England

Library of Congress Cataloging-in-Publication Data has been applied for.

ISBN: 978-0-06-123149-0
ISBN–10: 0-06-123149-5

Picture credits

Pages 9, 14, 20, 21, 22, 26, 32, 38, 42, 46, 55, 58, 71, 76, 78, 98, 107, 108, 109, 112,
115, 116, 126, 127 and 128 © Hulton-Deutsch Collection/CORBIS; pages 10,
12, 25, 31, 35, 44, 48, 60, 61, 63, 73, 90, 91, 99, 100, 102, 104 and 120
© Bettmann/CORBIS; pages 16, 52 and 121 © Olivier Martel/CORBIS; pages
19, 67 and cover and 94 © Marvin Koner/CORBIS; page 29 © Wally
McNamee/CORBIS; page 30 © Annie Griffiths Belt/CORBIS; page 37
© KOREN ZIV/CORBIS SYGMA; page 40 © E.O. Hoppé/CORBIS; page 50
© Michael Brennan/CORBIS; page: 57 © GOUPY DIDIER/CORBIS
SYGMA; pop up © Gary Houlder/CORBIS; page 68 © Yves Gellie/Corbis;
pages 72 and 97 © Julio Donoso/CORBIS SYGMA; page 74 and endpapers and
page 82 © CORBIS; pages 80 and 124 © Joseph Schwartz/CORBIS; page 85
© Sean Sexton Collection/CORBIS; page 86 © Stephanie Maze/CORBIS;
page 87 © Paul Kaye; Cordaiy Photo Library Ltd./CORBIS; page 88 © Geray
Sweeney/CORBIS; page 92 © Karen Tweedy-Holmes/CORBIS; page 110
© Thierry Prat/Sygma/Corbis; page 113 © Reuters/CORBIS; page 119 ©
Alinari Archives/CORBIS; page 122 © Minnesota Historical Society/CORBIS

Scary Nuns

HarperEntertainment

An Imprint of HarperCollins*Publishers*

Introduction

A nun, as defined by most common dictionaries, is a member of a religious order who is bound by vows of poverty, chastity, and obedience. Most Catholic schoolkids see them as furious, rosary-swinging automatons on wheels. To those countless Catholic schoolchildren as well as any number of non-Catholics, nuns are quite scary. This is not just because they are symbols of rigid discipline and harsh punishment administered swiftly, but because they are different from you and me—different in a wholly confusing way. For a start, nuns thrive on denial. They deny themselves not just the everyday pleasures of modern life, but also its basic pleasures—freedom, self-empowerment, sex, family life, and children, among them. They're secretive, live in closed societies, and still wear almost identical clothes (although different orders do have some unusual takes on the traditional black and white habits). They also make themselves completely servile to men who are similarly dedicated to vows of chastity (though not poverty), obedience to God, and wearing dresses in public.

To many of us born into our liberated, secular Western society, it is almost frightening that any woman similarly born would willingly take the archaic vows of a Catholic nun. And they truly are archaic.

It is claimed that nuns have existed since the day Mary Magdalen was first surprised to see Jesus out of His tomb. Before He was crucified women liked Jesus because He was far more of a feminist than other men of the time, and like any latter-day rock star, He attracted a following of teenage virgins. As with music legends, that following increased after His death, resurrection, and ascension. However, unlike generations of modern teenage virgins, women in the first centuries AD chose to follow the ways of Christ for the very good reason that if they did the work of the Church they could remain virgins and claim to be married (to Jesus), and thus avoid the unwanted attentions of men who believed that women were chattel.

In the early days of Christianity, Tertullianus (c. 150–220 AD), one of the founding fathers of the Latin Church, specified that only a virgin who had publicly taken her veil could be a nun—in fact, the veil that ceremoniously declared a nun's betrothal to Christ was the same as that worn by women who married men rather than the son of God. A century later, St. Athanasius, the self-styled Father of Orthodoxy and determined spreader of the Faith, wrote that nuns deserved to be considered the brides of Christ, and the name stuck.

During a nun's initiation service she pledges herself body and soul to the Lord, forsaking all others and takes on another name—usually that of a chosen saint or one of Jesus's disciples—so the marriage analogy is taken as far as it can. St. Cyprian, one of Athanasius's contemporaries, went as far as depicting virgin nuns who broke their vows as adulterers. For the rest of her life the "newlywed" will wear her "wedding" dress, which consists of a habit (a shapeless, usually rough-hewn cloth), wimple (the cloth worn around and over the top of the head), guimpe (the starched collar worn around the neck and over the shoulders), coif (the skullcap worn under the wimple), and flat sandals (though if she's a Discalced Carmelite she'll wear no shoes at all). Many orders of nuns still wear their wimples and habits in the style of medieval bridal gowns.

In the third century, the leaders of the Christian church organized the ladies into orders, often housing them in wings adjoined to monk-occupied monasteries. In addition to teaching the word of God (the word "nun" is derived from the French for tutor), the nuns did the washing, ironing, and cooking. This probably came as a bit of a shock to some, as they had opted for a life dedicated to God in order to avoid a life of servitude to a swine herder, when they found themselves doing everything (except the nasty) for a bunch of balding, fat drunks in sackcloths. (However, if you listen to some third-century serf gossip, the poor gals had to do the nasty, too. But those are claims that cannot be confirmed, along with allegations that they drank the blood of children and ate small babies for dinner.)

As hard as it may be to believe, there was a hint of feminism in the early lives of nuns. In the first few centuries after Christ, women—especially the poorer ones—had few life options, and fewer rights than a farm animal. Most of the common girls born before the Middle Ages were sold at a young age as a wife to any man who could afford a few bags of beans, half a pig, or a jug of ale. Many women were not educated unless they were aristocracy—and only then were they taught how to read the Bible, crochet, and order servants about. However, as part of a religious order, girls could avoid rape, learn to read, and command respect because they answered directly to a higher power.

But it wasn't only the poorer girls who became nuns. Starting in the Middle Ages, many rich men, aristocrats and royalty, sent their daughters to take the veil rather than have them claimed as wives by men who would demand a dowry, land, or power, as sons-in-law do. Princesses and duchesses were sent to convents at a young age in order to preserve their virginity (at least until their daddies could auction it to the highest bidder). Although nuns were pledged to a life of poverty, many medieval convents thrived on the bestowment of funds from these rich fathers. The Catholic Church was always hungry for cash to prettify the Vatican or build magnificent cathedrals, and so Church leaders would gladly accept monetary gifts in return for protecting an important hymen or two.

And that brings us to an all-important crux of the matter that makes nuns oh-so scary: sex (or the lack thereof). Today, after almost two millennia, a nun must be a virgin or at worst a widow (divorcées still cannot take the veil), for the very good reason that they are supposed to be as resistant to temptation as Jesus had been. We who delight in the sins of the flesh know that self-denial is far more harmful than self-abuse and cannot understand why anyone would willingly deny themselves sexual pleasure.

For those fearfully raised to believe that nuns quite eagerly refuse all earthly delights, the desire to comprehend that this is not the case can be immense, and images of nuns (or rather, actresses dressed in habits) enjoying sex have become a fetish of sorts around the world.

The idea of nuns enjoying sex or being tortured by sexual desire is not new. Movies have employed this sacrilegious concept for decades, perhaps in an attempt to humanize these women, or to shed light on their secretive ways. Among the most famous examples are *Black Narcissus* (1947); *The Devils* (1971); and two Italian classics, *Killer Nun* (1978) starring Anita Ekberg as a morphine-addicted nun, and *Flavia the Rebel Nun* (1974), in which a proto-feminist 16th-century nun runs away from her convent with a Jew and returns with a Muslim and his men to rape and ransack it.

Of course there are plenty of lighthearted movies that feature innocent nuns, with the nun often used as a symbol of naïveté, innocence, and fun. But even *The Singing Nun* (1966) has the main character, played by Debbie Reynolds, fighting sexual attraction to a man, and Julie Andrews's Maria in *The Sound of Music* (1964) ultimately renounces her vows when she falls for Baron von Trapp, demonstrating that moviegoers want to see that nuns have desires of the flesh just like everyone else.

More often than not though, the nun has come to represent something sinister. Many of us only have to see a nun to feel a shiver of fear run down our spine. Perhaps it is the long legacy of too many nuns shattering childhood innocence that earned all wimple-wearing women their woeful reputation. Perhaps it's that we will never truly understand these strange creatures who remove themselves from society. Just as likely though, it is because we live in a world where we cannot or will not believe in innate goodness in anyone.

Whether or not you were unlucky enough to have had rosary beads smacked across your knuckles by a rabid penguin, welcome to *Scary Nuns*. Read this book and be safe in the knowledge that you are not alone and it wasn't all a horrible dream. Although you will never know what goes on behind convent doors, conquer your fears with the knowledge that some secretive sisters take joy in modern activities like shooting guns, splashing in the sea, and hitting home runs. It seems that some girls just want to have fun, even if they are married to God.

So laugh, and get over it.

Peace be with you.

Come, pensive nun, devout and pure, sober steadfast, and demure, all in a robe of darkest grain, flowing with majestic train.

JOHN MILTON, IL PENSEROSO, C.1630

OPPOSITE A Carmelite nun reading by her bed, 1904.

NEXT PAGE The Sisters of Divine Providence try out the new .22-caliber guns presented to them by Harrington and Richardson. The guns would be used in a rifle training program at the camp, Massachusetts, 1957.

For my own part I believe no one on earth should be so happy as a nun.

Dame Laurentia McLachlan, Benedictine nun and Abbess of Stanbrook, 1931

Saint Ursula (probably third century AD), *leader of 11,000 virgins unto death*

Ursula's story is a sad and scary one. It is believed that she lived in the third century (or the fifth) and that she was a British princess and devout Christian nun who, in order to escape persecution at the hands of pagan peasants in her English homeland, traveled to France with 11,000 other virgins. Or it could have been 11. Unfortunately, the Huns invaded France soon after and, despising Christians, demanded Ursula and her 11,000 (or 11) followers renounce their faith. Ursula refused, as did her virgin entourage. As a result, the Huns shot and killed Ursula by arrow and beheaded her virgins. There is little doubt that many of them went to their graves with all limbs still intact. Ursula is now considered to be the welcoming presence at the gates of heaven, but only for virgins. Which, given that she caused 11,000 of them to be martyred, seems more than a little ironic.

OPPOSITE A nun gives a lesson to a class at a school for the blind, Germany, mid-20th century.

Something in that vast solitary garret sounded strangely. Most surely and certainly I heard, as it seemed, a stealthy foot on that floor: a sort of gliding out from the direction of the black recess haunted by the malefactor cloaks. I turned: my light was dim; the room was long—but as I live! I saw in the middle of that ghostly chamber a figure all black and white; the skirts straight, narrow, black; the head bandaged, veiled, white.

Say what you will, reader—tell me I was nervous or mad; affirm that I was unsettled by the excitement of that letter; declare that I dreamed; this I vow—I saw there—in that room—on that night—an image like—a NUN.

I cried out; I sickened. Had the shape approached me I might have swooned. It receded: I made for the door. How I descended all the stairs I know not.

CHARLOTTE BRONTË, VILLETTE, *1853*

PREVIOUS PAGE Nuns holding an illuminated baby Jesus during Candlemas, France, 2005.

ABOVE Carmelite nuns, including sisters and novices, walk in procession, France, 1904.

OPPOSITE Carmelite nuns farm in the fields. They wear the straw hats over their veils, which they never raise in public, France, 1904.

I wanted to be a nun. I saw nuns as superstars. . . .When I was growing up I went to a Catholic school, and the nuns, to me, were these superhuman, beautiful, fantastic people.

MADONNA, POP SINGER, 1986

OPPOSITE Arriving at Miami International Airport after expulsion from Cuba by Fidel Castro.

NEXT PAGE A Carmelite nun lies prostrate to expiate her sins, France, 1904.

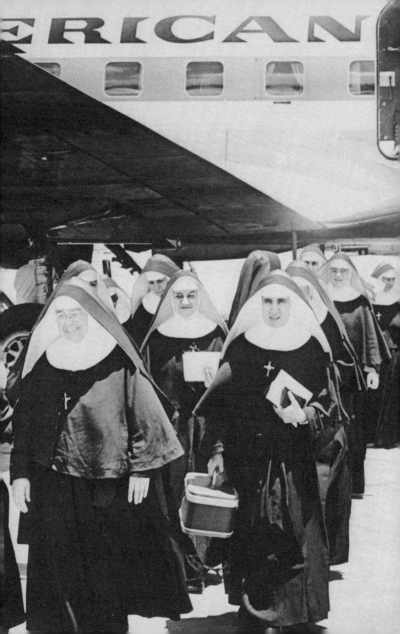

A nun, at best, is only half a woman, just as a priest is only half a man.

H. L. MENCKEN, WRITER, WIT AND CRITIC, 1956

ABOVE Nuns on television, Ireland, 1991.

OPPOSITE Sister Luelle Marie and Sister Mary Marlene go fishing, Wisconsin, 1965.

NEXT PAGE Nurses and nuns in an air raid shelter, France, 1940.

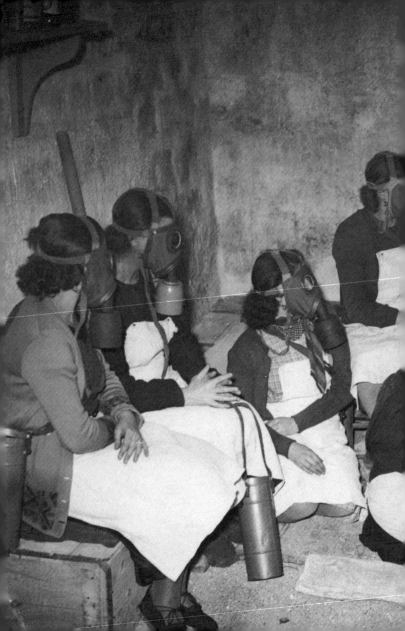

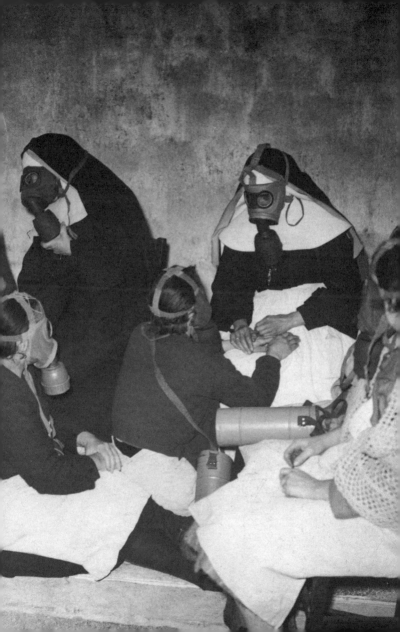

Teresa of Ávila (1515–1582), *founder of the Discalced Carmelites,*
who liked to whip herself when feeling "bad"

A religious little girl, Teresa ran away at the age of seven, intending
to persuade Moorish Muslims to cut her head off and make her
a martyr, but her plan was thwarted when a relative found the
imaginative child and returned her home. As a teenager she
joined the convent of Encarnación, on the edge of Ávila, and
immediately suffered a dramatic period of ill health. She lapsed
into a coma and on waking she remained paralyzed for almost a
year. During her recovery she began reading the works of Catholic
mystics, and quickly started having holy raptures, visions,
locutions, and levitations. In the convent, and across the Spanish
countryside, news of Teresa's divine aptitude spread fast. In 1562,
fed up with the gossip and frivolity of the Encarnación, she
founded a discalced (shoeless) convent in the middle of Ávila,
where she and her pure-minded followers wore sackcloths, slept
on straw pallets, and counted themselves lucky to have an egg
with their meager dinner. Beneath her habit, Teresa wore a hair
shirt (literally a rough, hairy, and uncomfortable cloth garment
designed to focus the penitent's mind on meditation and
suffering), stinging nettles for bracelets, and carried a scourge, her
disciplina, in case she felt she needed reproof, which was often.
Once, feeling that the scourge was not enough, Teresa put on a
halter and a saddle weighted with stones and was led by another
nun into the refectory on all fours. Saddles and stones couldn't
stop her increasingly frequent levitations, however—at

OPPOSITE *The Ecstasy of Saint Teresa* by Bernini, Santa Maria della Vittoria, Rome.

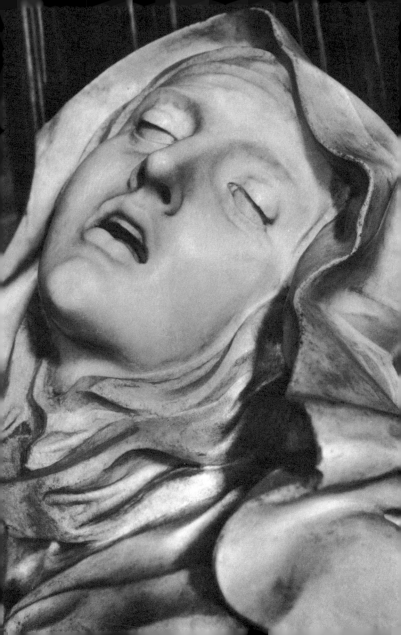

communion, she had to grip the altar grille to keep from scudding upward—her Carmelite sisters were put under standing orders to yank her down should she begin to float.

Teresa died in 1582 and was buried at the convent of Alba de Tormes. Not that a tomb could keep her down. When her grave was opened after a few months for inspection—an undecayed corpse indicated a candidate suitable for sainthood—her body was still intact and smelled of lilies. Various parts of her incorruptible body were cut off and distributed among her powerful admirers; her hand (minus a little finger) ended up with Generalissimo Franco of Spain in the 20th century, who kept it by his bed until his death. Teresa's heart rests in a case at the Alba convent and many people claim that there is a piercing in it, just where an angel could have pointed his spear.

OPPOSITE A nun kisses the stone where it is said that Christ's body was washed before burial, Jerusalem, 1999.

NEXT PAGE Carmelite nuns hold funeral mass for a sister, France, 1940.

Nuns fret not at their convent's narrow room;

And hermits are contented with their cells;

And students with their pensive citadels;

Maids at the wheel, the weaver at his loom,

Sit blithe and happy; bees that soar for bloom,

High as the highest Peak of Furness-fells,

Will murmur by the hour in foxglove bells:

In truth the prison, unto which we doom

Ourselves, no prison is: and hence for me,

In sundry moods, 'twas pastime to be bound

Within the Sonnet's scanty plot of ground;

Pleased if some Souls (for such there needs must be)

Who have felt the weight of too much liberty,

Should find brief solace there, as I have found.

WILLIAM WORDSWORTH, *1806*

LEFT A nun leads her charges to school during a Franco-era strike, Barcelona, 1951.

PREVIOUS PAGE Rehearsing for a charity fundraiser, Chicago, 1967.

NEXT PAGE Sister Mary Immaculate sits outside her home in Hempstead, New York, surrounded by religious artifacts with which she was dispossessed for nonpayment of rent, May 21, 1941. She had come from Berlin in 1928 to establish a missionary for other sisters who were to follow her. None came.

Playing snooker gives you firm hands and helps to build up character. It is the ideal recreation for dedicated nuns.

LUIGI BARBARITO, ARCHBISHOP AND PAPAL EMISSARY, 1989

Above The Sisters of St. Paul play pool in their convent, Brookline, Massachusetts, 2000.

Anne Catherine Emmerich (1774–1824), *an Augustinian stigmatic who was often found ecstatic, and sometimes clairvoyant*

Anne Catherine was born, lived, and died in poverty, but her visions and conversations with Jesus in Heaven and chats with poor souls suspended in Purgatory made her something of a celebrity in her native Germany. After being bedridden by visions and blinding headaches (it is likely that she had some kind of brain tumor), she recited her own version of Christ's last days, which she dubbed *The Dolorous Passion of Christ*, adding extra bits of blood and gore, and some anti-Semitic flourishes that the Bible failed to mention. Anne Catherine was never popular with her fellow nuns, however. They thought she listened in on their conversations, and couldn't stand it when she would "ghost" into a room; the other sisters would find her behind them without having heard her walk in, which they naturally thought was her annoying ability to materialize at will. Anne Catherine was also prone to bleeding from her palms and small wounds on her chest (in the same spot where a Roman soldier's spear supposedly pierced the heart of Jesus while He hung on the Cross). These bloody marks would appear after Anne Catherine's clairvoyant pronouncements about people she'd never met. Yes, she was clairvoyant, too.

PREVIOUS PAGE Prayers at the convent of the Sacred Heart of Jesus, France.

RIGHT A Carmelite nun at prayer, France, 1992.

ABOVE Mother Cabrini (1850–1917), the first American to be canonized, posing in her nun's habit.

OPPOSITE Mother Mary Katherine Drexel, the world's richest nun, died at the age of 96 after giving all her money away.

PREVIOUS PAGE A group of English nuns enjoy a smoke.

Bernadette Soubirous of Lourdes *(1844–1879),*
the nun who wouldn't lie down

At the tender age of 14, Bernadette Soubirous saw the Virgin Mary in a cave near Lourdes and reported the meeting. Naturally, she was called a liar. A couple of weeks later, when water started to trickle out of the same cave, it was reported to have healing properties and Bernadette was proclaimed a true visonary. The cave became an annual pilgrimage site for the sick and lame. Unfortunately, the waters didn't heal Bernadette, who suffered from severe asthma and, bizarrely, tuberculosis of the right kneebone, which kept her bedridden for the rest of her short life. The Sisters of Nevers, her local convent, moved her in and cared for her until her death in 1879. As with her saintly predecessors, her coffin was dug up a few decades later to see if she'd turned into compost. The opened casket revealed a still intact body which the nuns washed and then reburied. In 1919 Bernadette was dug up again, and was once more found to be in pretty good condition for a woman who had been dead for 40 years. She was reburied, but in 1925 she rose again a third and final time (why is that so familiar?). She stayed up and is still on display in the chapel at the Church of St. Gildard. That's not her real face, though—it's a wax mask that was made in 1925.

RIGHT St. Bernadette of Lourdes, photo circa 1876.

Sister Maria Jesus Agreda (1602–1665), *the original Flying Nun, aka The Blue Nun*

As a teenage novice in Spain, Maria meditated for hours, sometimes all day. In the evening she'd tell stories to fellow sisters about the spiritual travels she'd made to faraway lands, meeting savages and spreading the Word of Christ. Maria wrote a book describing in great detail her missionary work among the savages of The New World, without ever having left her convent. At the time there was a little thing called The Inquisition going on in her homeland, and Maria was called to a public trial. In the middle of it, just as things were looking very bad for her, a band of conquistadors and friars returned from a region north of Mexico, where they had encountered Native American tribes who had already been converted to Christianity, and somehow knew of Jesus Christ the Savior. The Indians claimed they had been visited by a white-skinned "Blue Lady" who appeared to them drifting in a blue haze in the sky, and preached the Word of the Lord in their native languages. Case closed, Maria was acquitted of heresy as it was proved she could indeed astrally project herself to the other side of the world. Even after three centuries, it turns out, Sister Maria Jesus Agreda is incorruptible. The flush of her cheeks and her life-like features still baffle the Catholic Church and modern science today: her coffin was last opened in 1989 by a medical doctor who proclaimed that her body was in the same condition as had been reported at the previous opening in 1909.

RIGHT A nun watches children sleep at Casa de Beneficencia Orphanage in Havana, Cuba, 1955.

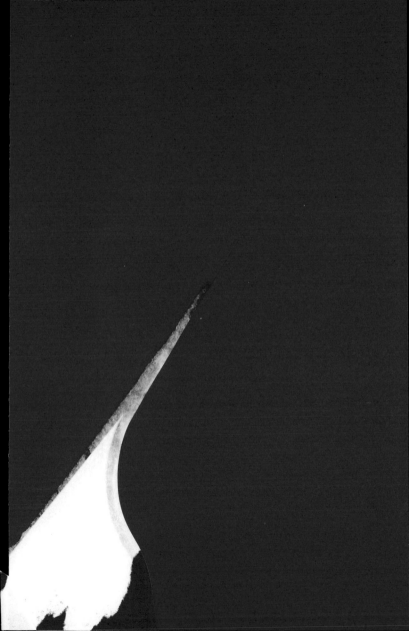

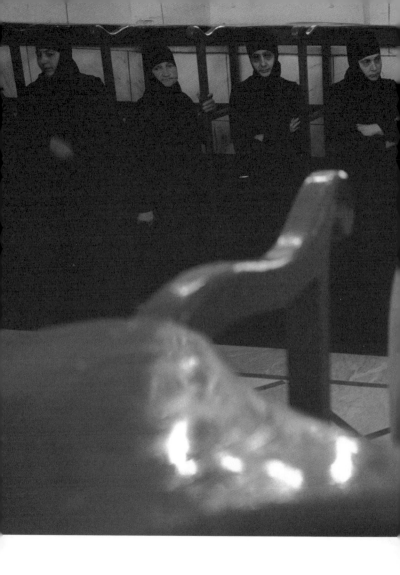

ABOVE Prayers in the church of Saidnaya Convent, Syria, 2005.

If you ever walk past a nun, immediately touch a piece of iron, or say "Your nun!" to a passerby—passing any bad luck to them.

ITALIAN SUPERSTITION

She gave up beauty in her tender youth, gave all her hope and joy and pleasant ways; she covered up her eyes lest they should gaze on vanity, and chose the bitter truth.

Christina Rossetti, Portrait of her sister, a Nun, c. 1860

OPPOSITE A blind girl touches the face of a nun at a school for blind children run by Franciscan nuns, Warsaw, Poland, 1989.

ABOVE Shooting at bull's-eyes, Palisades Amusement Park, New Jersey, 1962.

NEXT PAGE Sisters of the Holy Family gather for a portrait. The photograph, taken in New Orleans, Louisiana, in 1900, was shown at the Paris Exposition in an exhibit of African American life.

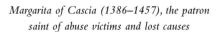

Margarita of Cascia (1386–1457), the patron saint of abuse victims and lost causes

Rita was betrothed to an abusive town watchman named Paolo Mancini. She bore him twin sons and suffered physical abuse at his hands until 1422, when he was stabbed to death in an ambush. Shortly after, her sons, who had inherited their father's abusive streak, swore vengeance on his killers. Rita appealed to Heaven that they would not achieve success in revenge, and God responded—the brothers both died within the year. Rita promptly moved into the local convent at Cascia, where she stayed for 34 years, during the last 15 of which her head bled constantly, the wounds appearing as if she had been wearing a crown of thorns. For the final four years of her life Rita was reported to have been bedridden (most likely to do with significant loss of blood), and would only consume the Eucharist (that is, bread and water). Naturally Rita became the patron saint of no-hopers because her life turned out so well after quite a dreadful beginning.

LEFT The corpse of a Carmelite nun on public display in Spain, during the Spanish Civil War, Barcelona, 1936.

Nuns and married women are equally unhappy, if in different ways.

CHRISTINA OF SWEDEN, SCANDINAVIAN MONARCH, 17TH CENTURY

OPPOSITE Commuting on the A train, New York, 1940s.

NEXT PAGE Sister Mary Aquinas Kinsky, the "flying nun," teaches practical radio operations to sisters attending her Civil Aeronautics Authority course at Catholic University, Washington, D.C., 1943.

...And behind this a nun was standing. Her countenance, which showed her to be about twenty-five years old, gave the impression, at a first glance, of beauty, but of beauty worn, faded, and, one might almost say, spoiled. A black veil, stiffened and stretched quite flat upon her head, fell on each side and stood out a little way from her face; under the veil, a very white linen band half covered a forehead of different but not inferior whiteness; a second band, in folds, down each side of the face, crossed under the chin, encircled the neck, and was spread a little over the breast to conceal the opening of a black dress.

ALESSANDRO MANZONI, I PROMESSI SPOSI (THE BETROTHED), *1842*

OPPOSITE Nun in full habit, Ireland, late 19th century.

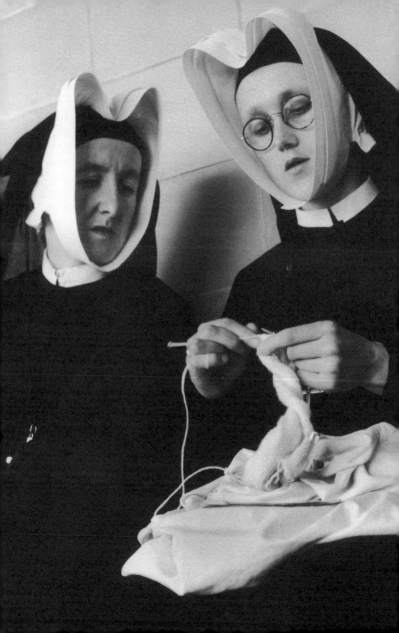

If the monks and nuns are not living a life of constant prayer, or at least striving toward that, then their lives are a waste and a scandal. Let the monastery be sold and the money given to the poor.

Fr. M. Basil Pennington, *abbot and writer, 1966*

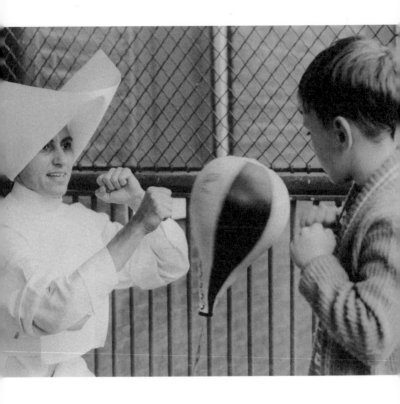

ABOVE Sister Teresa Joseph teaches her six-year-old student to box, St. Louis, Missouri, 1961.

OPPOSITE Sister Euphemia and Sister Michael James ride the Tomorrowland rocket at Disneyland, California, 1962.

PREVIOUS PAGE Dolls in a souvenir shop window, Ireland, 2002.

Catherine of Siena (1347–1380), *who liked to catch falling heads and bathe in blood*

Always a devoted girl, Catherine gave herself to Christ at age seven, and by the time she was 16 she had already experienced celestial visitations and had several chats with Him.

In the summer of 1370 she went into a dream-like state for a few weeks, during which she claimed that God took her on a tour of Hell, Purgatory, and Heaven, and then asked her to spread His Word. So she did, through a series of letters to various princes, merchants, and criminals. Niccolo di Toldo received one of Catherine's letters in his cell as he was waiting to be beheaded and he asked her to come to his execution. She got the best seat in the house—on the executioner's scaffold, no less—as she explained in a letter to Blessed Raymond of Capua: "I have just taken a head into my hands and have been moved so deeply that my heart cannot grasp it . . . I waited for [Niccolo] at the place of execution . . . he arrived like a meek lamb and when he saw me he began to smile. He asked me to make the Sign of the Cross over him . . . I stretched out his neck and bent down to him, reminding him of the blood of the Lamb. His lips kept murmuring only 'Jesus' and 'Catherine,' and he was still murmuring when I received his head into my hands . . . my soul rested in peace and quiet, so aware of the fragrance of blood that I could not remove the blood which had splashed onto me."

OPPOSITE Catherine of Siena, the Vatican, Rome.

Myra Babbitt—Mrs. George F. Babbitt—was definitely mature. She had creases from the corners of her mouth to the bottom of her chin, and her plump neck bagged. But the thing that marked her as having passed the line was that she no longer had reticences before her husband, and no longer worried about not having reticences. She was in a petticoat now, and corsets which bulged, and unaware of being seen in bulgy corsets. She had become so dully habituated to married life that in her full matronliness she was as sexless as an anemic nun.

SINCLAIR LEWIS, BABBITT, *1922*

RIGHT Franciscan nuns share a Bible at an educational center for blind children in Warsaw, Poland, 1989.

OPPOSITE Two nuns operating a water hose, mid–20th century.

ABOVE Getting a better view of St. Peter's Basilica and the crowd in St. Peter's Square for Marian Year ceremonies, Vatican City, 1954.

ABOVE AND OPPOSITE Ice-skating nuns, at first off to a good start, find it a bit too slippery as a few take a spill on the ice. Some 24 nuns were guests of the Belleville Serra Club for an ice-skating party. Although the sisters ended up in many a collision, they took to the sport with good humor, Illinois, 1965.

Theseus to Hermia:

Either to die the death, or to abjure

For ever the society of men.

Therefore, fair Hermia, question your desires;

Know of your youth, examine well your blood,

Whether, if you yield not to your father's choice,

You can endure the livery of a nun,

For aye to be in shady cloister mew'd,

To live a barren sister all your life,

Chanting faint hymns to the cold fruitless moon.

Thrice blessed they that master so their blood,

To undergo such maiden pilgrimage;

But earthlier happy is the rose distill'd,

Than that which withering on the virgin thorn

Grows, lives, and dies, in single blessedness.

WILLIAM SHAKESPEARE, A MIDSUMMER NIGHT'S DREAM, ACT 1, SCENE 1, MID-1590s

OPPOSITE Sister Magdalene of San Antonio, Texas, steps in determinedly to slam the ball in a ball game at the Davenport Ranch, Austin, Texas, 1963.

Convent: A place of retirement for women who wish for leisure to meditate upon the sin of idleness.

AMBROSE BIERCE, WRITER, 1881

OPPOSITE Beguine sisters in Mother Superior's room in a Netherlands convent, 1955.

PREVIOUS PAGE In a traffic jam on a bumper cars ride at the Chicago Free Fair, 1962.

When I was a little girl, I used to dress my Barbie in a nun's habit so she could beat the hell out of Skipper and not get in trouble for it.

BRYNN HARRIS, COMEDIAN, 2005

Order of the Poor Clares (1212–present),
not the greatest babysitters

Saint Clare of Assisi received her habit from Saint Frances of Assisi himself in 1212, and today the Poor Clare nuns live and work all over the world. In Ireland they will forever be associated with tragedy, however. One night in February 1943, a fire broke out in a County Cavan orphanage for girls, killing 35 children and one adult. An inquiry into the fire blamed outside factors such as an ill-equipped fire service, but locals believed more lives would have been saved had the nuns not been so concerned that they and the girls would be seen in their nightclothes. There were also rumors that the sisters locked their charges up—and even tied them to their beds to prevent them from wandering after lights out, further preventing emergency evacuation.

OPPOSITE Virginia McKenna as the convent prioress in John Whiting's play *The Devils*, England, 1964.

PREVIOUS PAGES (LEFT) Sister Augusta helps to dress a five-year-old who plays the Dresden Shepherdess in a Christmas sketch at the Guardian Angels School, England, 1937. (RIGHT) An actress dressed like a nun parades in front of visitors of Germany's first Ecumenical Church Congress in Berlin, 2003.

The experiment, called the Nun Study, is considered by experts on aging to be one of the most innovative efforts to answer questions about who gets Alzheimer's disease and why.

For 15 years, elderly Catholic nuns have had their genes analyzed and balance and strength measured. They have been tested on how many words they can remember minutes after reading them on flashcards, how many animals they can name in a minute, and whether they can count coins correctly.

The autobiographical essays they wrote for their order in their twenties, when they took their vows, have been scrutinized, their words plumbed for meaning. And as they have died, their brains have been removed and shipped in plastic tubs to a laboratory where they are analyzed and stored in jars.

THE JOURNAL OF PERSONALITY AND SOCIAL PSYCHOLOGY, *MAY 2001*

OPPOSITE A nun from the Russian Compound strolling in the Holy Land, 1950.

Sisters Adorers of the Precious Blood (1861–present),
who wear blood-red robes

The Order of the Sisters Adorers of the Precious Blood was founded in 1861, in Saint Hyacinth, Canada, by Mother Catherine-Aurelia, who had a thing for blood, it seems. One Quebec bishop claimed that he saw blood coming from her forehead. Several witnesses reported seeing blood moisten the fabric around her heart, while others claimed that her dress miraculously changed from black to white, then to red, which should have given rise to the old joke: What's black, white, red, and can't turn around in a corridor? (A: a nun with a javelin in her hand.) Today the Sisters wear a red vest over white robes in memory of their founder. Rumors that they drink real blood are unfounded.

The convent, which belongs to the West as it does to the East, to antiquity as it does to the present time, to Buddhism and Muhammadanism as it does to Christianity, is one of the optical devices whereby man gains a glimpse of infinity.

Victor Hugo, writer and dramatist, 1862

Above A nun with a crown of thorns prays with other hooded nuns at the Convent of the Sacred Heart of Jesus, France.

Opposite Portrait of a nun with a young orphan, 1900s.

Rosalind: And his kissing is as full of sanctity as the touch of holy bread.

Celia: He hath bought a pair of cast lips of Diana: a nun of winter's sisterhood kisses not more religiously; the very ice of chastity is in them.

WILLIAM SHAKESPEARE; As You Like It, *ACT III, SCENE IV, 1599*

OPPOSITE Waiting for a streetcar on 7th Street, Los Angeles, 1950s.

PREVIOUS PAGE Orphans pose with a nun at Christmas in Minnesota, 1900s.

ABOVE Members of the Ghent Béguinage at dinner.

OPPOSITE Convent caters for weddings, England, 1960s.

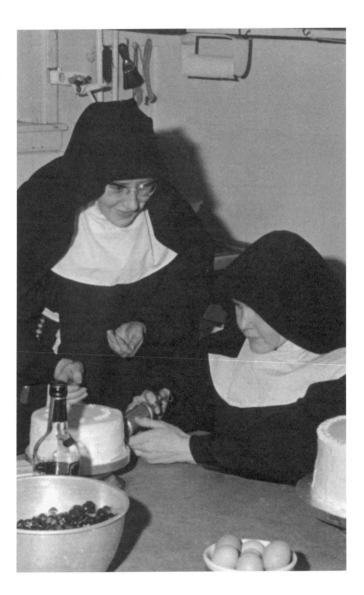